Faceless Love

by
Byron Simmons

DORRANCE
PUBLISHING CO
EST. 1920
PITTSBURGH, PENNSYLVANIA 15238

Cover Art By: David Aaron Craig

Dorrance Publishing Co
585 Alpha Drive
Pittsburgh, PA 15238
Visit our website at www.dorrancebookstore.com

ISBN: 979-8-8860-4020-3
eISBN: 979-8-8860-4925-1

Dedication

I dedicate Faceless Love to all those in love, in need of love, or on the search for love. May this assist you on your path one way or another, whether it inspires you to love harder or activates the love you have deep within yourself. I hope you find love as pure as it may come for if nobody else loves you, I do.

I also would like to take the time to give a special thank you to a handful of people that have helped and supported me along my process of writing poetry. The first group of people being my family, thank you for supporting me all these years in finding my gift of writing and helping me improve every day. I want to thank my coworkers; D'Anna Coleman, Raquel Towers (and her family), Nicole Patton, David Craig, Joseph Connor III, Amber Graham, and Javier Morales. Three years ago, this young, foolish kid entered your guys' life and played around with poetry until the moment you spoke to him about showing it to the world. Most importantly you guys gave me another place to call home. Now three years later after you constantly staying on my case about getting my work out there, WE FINALLY DID IT! All of you have become like family to me and I want to give a special thank you to you for supporting me and embracing like one of your own it means the world to me. I also want to thank my friends who have helped and supported me. Unfortunately, I can't name you all because I don't want to exclude anybody who was there but know you are appreciated more than you know, and I love you all. <u>Faceless Love</u> is a book dedicated to all of you, my fallen angels both family and friends,

Table of Contents

Page 1	Love Me Naked
Page 2	A Letter To You
Page 3	A Three Letter Word
Page 4	A Whisper In The Wind
Page 5	A White Heart And A Blue Mind; 3 AM
Page 6	And If We Never Speak Again
Page 7	Before We Go
Page 8	Can I Come Home
Page 9	Don't Forget Me
Page 10	Don't Leave The Light On
Page 11	For Tonight
Page 12	Here's My Answer
Page 13	I Fell In Love
Page 14	I Had A Dream Yesterday
Page 15	I Love You
Page 16-17	I Never Would've Guessed
Page 18	I Want To Hear It
Page 19	If This World Were Mine
Page 20	It Was Just A Kiss
Page 21	Late At Night; A Concept
Page 22	2 Love Me Naked
Page 23	Love Desires
Page 24	Love Has A Sound
Page 25	Lov3 M3 Nak3d
Page 26	Love Me 4 Me
Page 27	Love Poem: The Story
Page 28-29	Maybe I'm Overqualified
Page 30	My Love Poem Would Sound Like
Page 31-32	Not So Simple
Page 33	One Night In Love
Page 34	Some Words
Page 35	The First Day
Page 36-37	The Love Poem
Page 38	The Outer Body Experience
Page 39	The Sight Of You
Page 40-41	The Stoplight
Page 42	We Are Peace
Page 43-44	What You Mean To Me
Page 45-46	When The Love Runs Deep
Page 47	You
Page 48	A Faceless Love

Take a minute to let the wind speak,
My heart has a few words to say,
And I hope you don't allow your ears to shrink,
Because if I didn't tell you before, I want you to love me naked,
If it's not too much to ask, I'm an introvert, so everything goes down to
    the basics,
Like how I loved a girl and still got told I was the reason her wrists were
    to bleed,
And how I gave my heart to the wrong person one too many times and
    they stepped on me,
But I'm not asking for sympathy, so please don't feel sorrow,
I want you to love me naked,
Meaning you can hear every word I'm saying and love me the same to-
    morrow,
I like to love hard because love is like the dollar you don't have to pay
    back,
I'm not asking you to be a cardiologist, I just want you to fill in the cracks,
Because they told me I wouldn't make it to this point,
She told me she loved me, but it burnt faster than any joint,
I want you to love me naked,
My wish has always been to set my heart into somebody's hands without
    them wanting to break it

I know you're somewhere out there,
And if you, are I hope that you're listening,
I've spent the last 547 days trying to figure out the one thing my life has
    been missing,
After all that time I found out that what I was missing was you,
Because on the day we first met it wasn't just your smile that told me you
    were beautiful,
So here I stand before your eyes conjuring my love letter for the days,
Now you may not know my name, but everybody knows about the rose
    in the case,
This time I placed my heart with it so that a true love could be frozen in place,
Because I haven't stopped thinking about how it'll all melt away the day
    I hear your name,
There's been so many days and nights where I'd sit there dreaming about
    you being next to me,
Honest to God one time I got so lost in thought I ended up in the wrong week,
I consider myself a hopeless romantic because I'm in to all the mushy,
    gushy things,
I dream that one day I'll be able to treat you to dinner and take you shopping,
Not casually, but for party dresses and wedding rings,
I want to have the best time of my life with you in a roller-skating rink,
And even if my dream is so far out of reach it is make-believe,
I'll make a night with you feel like a movie scene,
There's going to be smiles on both of our faces while everybody else
    watches two adults in love dancing,
I can change your life in the best way, please just hold my heart and take
    care of it,
I have unpleasant habits that'll make you want to hit the road, but to you
    I'll be a gentleman,
My name is Byron and I'll love you in whatever way you desire, it's kind
    of my specialty,
I may look tough on the outside, but I love it when you love me delicately

You,

A three-letter word describing the most beautiful woman ever created,

A three-letter word that I think of when I want pure greatness,

Spelled as a word it is Y-O-U,

Also, a member of the alphabet following being t is the simple letter u,

You are the most beautiful goddess I have ever seen,

On your worst day I honestly believe you could replace Aphrodite,

Under most circumstances you can find me in the back of the crowd hiding,

I spelled you in three lines, still whispering these words hoping you can
    find me,

Because right now feels like you're a thousand miles away in a different
    city,

So, I've started to yell what you need to hear, which is *tonight you look
    so pretty,*

I met you years ago and I loved you then, although I couldn't tell you so,

I guess I was wondering if my heart would still fit in my chest if I let it grow,

All right, I'm done hiding,

My heart was waiting for you to say that you won't let go,

I've written a thousand poems hoping you'd catch one line and let it be
    known,

I think if I was able to read what I wrote, you'd stay around to see if it
    were true,

Because it's not just a love poem this time,

This time I had to make it about you

I will find you again,
I will love you forever and always,
And for years I've been whispering it into the wind,
Hoping one day you'll realize the story of us doesn't end,
Hoping that when the sun rises on this day, I'll finally have the con-
    fidence,
The confidence to tell you how I feel before you decide to leave,
Because the sun is coming down and there's something else, I must con-
    fess to feel free,
I spent years writing you poems and love letters,
Hoping that as my skills develop so will your love for me because the
    words got cleverer,
When I first saw you the feeling I had was something I kept discreet,
Because when I looked into your eyes there was something about your
    love that made me drop all my groceries,
It had me stumbling around the supermarket as if I had two left feet,
The moment I got a taste of your love I knew I would become a fiend,
It's got me going crazy, thinking like the person standing next to me,
And whenever I listen to him, he says the craziest things,
But I voice them sometimes and they sound like insecurities,
I don't mean to come off that way, but I have this fear of the day you de-
    cide to leave,
I would've told you all this before but due to my poetic nature I'm shy,
My words translate better in audios rather than ears and eyes,
I always wanted to tell you I love you, but I didn't want to bore you with
    an ordinary message,
So, I'm leaving this here in hopes that you'll get it

Here's a message from this blue heart I never want you to forget about,
Because behind this smile lies nights of intoxication thinking about blow-
  ing my brains out,
I don't have to be in a speaker, but I desire to become one,
I want to turn my voice so loud they have no choice but to hear me,
Because these pills can't hide all the pain,
And this appearance is turning into the worst disguise,
I'm not a weak person, but I don't want to live in this world tainted with lies,
I mean I just want real love,
The kind where they can grab my hand and never let go,
And realize behind the pain you see, there is a soul made of gold,
I haven't been friends with happiness since I was about sixteen,
I cry and pound on my head, but these kinds of things I keep discreet,
Because I'm not sure if you're here for me or if you'll be gone next week,
It doesn't even matter to you, but they left without saying goodbye,
I'm not asking you to make up for what they did,
I'm just trying to find the reason why,
And I can never seem to find the answer, meaning this river of tears will
  never run dry,
Because it wasn't just an ex, it was her and my family combined,
And honestly if you were to say you don't care, you'd fall in line,
I'm saying this because nobody else wanted to hear everything I had to say,
They wanted to cut me off to say they understand before the end,
But if you understood you wouldn't be mad at me for being who I am

This may be my last declaration of love to you,
Although I hope it isn't because saying the last time always makes me
    uncomfortable,
I know you'll sweep it under the rug while I cover up my emotions like
    I always do,
Just know that no matter how you feel about me I will always love you,
I mean exactly how you expect the sun to come out and shine a little bit
    right before you see the moon,
It's still crazy when I think about how I won't be able to look at my phone
    screen to see you,
And if we never speak again,
I couldn't admit it, but you became my best friend,
And if this is the last time we speak,
I want you to know you showed me the world in a different light, an ex-
    perience I may never repeat,
But if you need me know that I'm still holding out my hand,
Waiting for you to return home although it may never happen again,
I want you to know my heart will forever cry just to be in your arms,
Because they all don't think I know what true love is, but I felt it this time
    praying it'll happen again,
And if we never speak again, know that I love you beyond human com-
    prehension,
For your name will forever be in my veins and time will tell if our love
    ever sees perfection,
We're separated by states yet drawn together by fatal attraction,
Simply two broken people trying to spark one heart into the realm of
    satisfaction,
But if we never speak again, I'll hold your name sky-high because the
    love from me will never be dead,
I hope this isn't the last time I hear your voice, but please stay safe and
    protected

I forgot to tell you how beautiful you are before you left today,
But in this I found the opportunity to show you that I'm a poet in a special
    kind of way,
And the only way I can start is by saying that I'm so in love with you,
If you were to express any of your dreams, I would work until it came true,
Because there's something about hearing your voice that makes my knees
    weak,
And the feeling of your touch has lifted me off my feet,
I'm sure you've heard plenty of people say this to you, but you can have
    anything,
I mean from a simple five-star meal in a beautiful setting to a wedding ring,
Sometimes I think to myself if only you knew the way I think about you,
I'm worshipping a goddess who just a few minutes ago was someone I
    never knew,
The thought of you never leaves my mind like I got a brain tattoo,
But if only you knew the way I feel about you,
You couldn't fathom the thought of leaving if you felt the way I do,
I smile when your name pops up on my phone because talking to you is
    my favorite thing to do,
I'm not here to apply to simply be a lover or best friend,
I want to be both of those and the person you spend the rest of your life with,
Because it was just a hug to you, but for me it was where my life began,
I want to teach you the concept of true love with better comparisons,
Where I close my eyes, and I dream that you're the only person I'll ever
    wake up with,
And before I go to sleep, you'll be the very last person to give me a good
    night's kiss,
Because eventually we'll turn old and gray, so deep in love with a few kids,
Maybe if you see this, you'll hear the obsession in my confession,
Before I go you should know you're the most beautiful woman I know,
And I'll have all the love in my heart fresh on the stove by the time you
    get home

I might sound crazy for asking this,
But can I come back home,
I'm asking you because home is where the heart is,
And if you are human, it should be in your chest,
But yours seems restless,
Like maybe it's been broken a couple times,
With a ninety percent chance of unexplainable wasted investments,
The only reason I'm saying this is because I looked in your eyes,
Instantly I was hypnotized, so I had to let you know I'm paying attention,
However, I want to let you know it was merely something I noticed,
But the topic is you, and that is where I'm focused,
I love whatever you feel like your flaws are regardless of whatever sins,
Because when it comes to you, I feel the need to give unconditional a
    definition,
My heart rests securely with you and I can say that with all confidence,
And I've had you once before which means I can't let you go again,
Even though it was a dream, the feeling it gave me was ever so lucid,
I felt your soul touch mine and soul ties are no illusion,
I should get back on topic since I've drawn out some confusion,
Home is where the heart is and my heart is at rest when I'm with you,
I mentioned your heart because it's been on my mind since minute
    number two,
Honestly, I pictured this ending with us walking into some random apart-
    ment and deciding to call it home,
Because whenever I'm writing about you my heart becomes warm

I really do love you, I feel it deep I my soul,
Every time I close my eyes, I imagine myself holding you and I never
 want to let you go,
And I can't let you leave because I've been here plenty of times before,
If you plan to leave you can find me six feet beneath the floor,
I'm scared to accept your love because every time I got comfortable, I
 got it wrong,
But after years of drowning in sorrows I know your love is what my heart
 was waiting on,
You never even knew that you were the only person to see me when I
 thought I was invisible,
I love the way you look me in my eyes, because for the first time I felt
 something that wasn't physical,
I tried explaining this to my friends the other night and they said whatever
 I was trying to say was crazy,
And now that I'm saying it aloud, I want to know what it is that you're
 doing to me,
But you make me want to paint the picture of love as if I was Leonardo
 da Vinci,
It may take a few years for me to open up and show you the real me,
You make me want to expose you to all my fears while I explain all my
 reasons,
I want to help you understand what makes me who I am and show you
 all these demons,
And I want you to know these words have been years in the making,
To me this is really love, which makes it easier for me to create the painting,
For this first time, I feel like I can talk to her and no matter what, she gets me,
I don't want to wake up until the day she finally comes to hug and kiss me,
You don't understand it's not just her touch, it's the way she looks at me
 that I'm missing,
I guess what I'm trying to ask is if you can let me in your heart and never
 forget me

I am an overthinker who has learned to be terrified of dark places,
Because the water will overflow the room making it hard to breathe in
    tight places,
These thoughts make it possible to drown in knee-high water without in-
    toxication,
But this time I want you to enter my mind,
So please don't leave the light on when you walk out that door,
Lately I've had the gut feeling of an angel showing themselves disguised
    with devil horns,
You may think I'm crazy,
But the other day she whispered that she was scared too,
And it was because she couldn't see the sky,
So, I stared as hard as I could to see the pain hidden behind her eyes,
And her wings were so beautiful, though I'm looking beyond them to see
    what I can find,
In the process of looking, I happened to find love,
Not only because I saw and accepted her pain,
More so because inaudibly learning about her let me know everything
    was going to be okay,
So don't leave that light on when you exit from this room,
I'm nyctophobic, but with her I feel like I'm at home,
This angel just happened to meet me at the worst time,
So, I want to show her that I'm more than fear and terrors,
I'm insecurity wrapped inside the body of some guy,
And I promise not to let them come in between us,
Because the gap in the clouds represents the space left for you and I,
I would like for you to be my pair of wings so we can make it up there tonight,
And I wrote this during my darkest hour without a sense to fight,
I like to think of myself as a moonflower,
Meaning you'll see the most beautiful side of me at night,
I think about her all the time even after the sunrise,
So please don't leave that light on, there's a place I have to be tonight

Faceless Love

You can wipe the tears from your face now because tonight I'm yours,
I'm willing to give you the best version of life that you adore,
Because I was up last night,
And for some reason the only thing I could think about was life with you,
I can't give it up because this dream is the only one that became a reality,
If love at first sight is really a thing,
I loved you way before I ever knew you,
You were faceless in my dream, but this feeling tells me it's you,
The world is a different place for you, it's better than the outdoors,
Because starting tonight, I'm all yours,
And I don't like the people I love crying,
I take it very personal, and if you ask anybody else, I'm not lying,
Maybe I'm saying too much, but honestly, I just don't want to lose you,
I've been hurt so bad before, and my heart is already sore,
And I know you've been hurt before too, but it's not like that anymore,
Honestly, I believe in soul ties,
And the other night I heard my soul cry for yours,
I'm not sure if it's the vibe I got from your presence,
I'm not even sure if you said hi back, I was lost in your essence,
Because true beauty is such a gift and you have the present,
It's wrapped inside the heart you keep hidden from the world,
You're such a gift to the universe, like literally the perfect girl,
As far as flaws, you have none, and that's why I wish to be yours,
I may be begging even though my intentions are pure,
If nobody else is, I'm more than ready to show you how great you are,
Way beyond just my heart, you alone are my shooting star,
Everything I wished for in the world was spotted within you by my heart,
All these thoughts just to say, "Hello, I'm Byron" and hope a
    conversation starts

11

I want to wake up with you in my arms,
The world is truly that much different whenever you're next to me,
I plan to be the first and last man to completely understand you sexually,
It's every moment we share on FaceTime that amplifies the electricity,
And I'm still wondering how a woman like you could be so into me,
You have me questioning if love can really be a thing,
With a follow-up of how far I can fall before I realize there was supposed
    to be somebody there to catch me,
And you're really a goddess in my eye,
I know you don't believe me when I say this, but you're the first angel I
    have ever seen,
I'm amazed by the smile on your face after all the pain and suffering,
You are the embodiment of power and the representation of a queen,
And I've never felt this way about anybody before,
Like butterflies in my stomach every time I go to open my mouth,
And I'll read you this poem one day hoping only the perfect words come out,
One thing I want you to know is that my phone is always on, so if you
    need me, feel free to give it a ring,
How do I feel about you?
I want you to stick around like all my tattoos,
In other words, permanently

I fell in love with you more than just once,
And every time you smile it warms my heart like the morning sun,
It was the first time I heard your voice that I fell in love,
And I knew I wanted to marry you the first time you gave me a hug,
I want you to know I think of you the same way Dorothy thought of Kansas,
The way I feel for you is so strong it could pull together all the planets,
I could go with the traditional "roses are red and violets are blue,"
But when I think of a three-letter word all I can come up with is you

I had a dream yesterday,
And to no surprise it was about you,
The first time I saw your face it was in the moon,
Controlling the tide of my emotion, establishing a power over me that
    you never even knew,
But after having this dream, it's safe to say my heart chose you,
In this dream I saw a woman beyond beautiful with movements so elegant,
And it wasn't until you turned and showed your face that I was able to
    make sense of it,
This woman would make you see the future while making love feel effortless,
You watch her control the world with her walk,
And her head held so high the only person she could be is miss independent,
If they ask me how I'm feeling, I could only tell them *desperate,*
Because I'm in love with you so I need you to focus on the predicate,
So, I'm just desperate to be in your arms, put a ring around your finger,
    and smile while your name hangs from my necklace,
The only word I can use to describe a moment with you is precious,
And I said I love you asking you to pay attention to the predicate,
Because when I'm in love I show it through actions displaying proper
    etiquette,
And I'm not sure if God took out one of my ribs or a piece of my heart
    when he made you for me,
He's made you more than a want,
You're everything my heart could ever need,
I used to beg all the time to feel love and be happy,
But now that I've found my place with you, all I feel is peace and serenity

When I feel the strongest, I have the hardest time finding out what to say,
I love you becomes a tongue twister in the most painful of ways,
So I'll say hi instead of how was your day,
At times it'll seem like I don't care, and it's been one of my worst mistakes,
Because I care about you so much even though it'll barely find its way
    onto my face,
Which is why the first time I saw you I couldn't find the confidence to
    ask for your name,
I looked into your eyes and saw everything love can be,
I saw here and now but a little more futuristically,
Inside my head I was scrambling for words while thinking there was no
    need to rush,
It's time to act like I've been here before because I'm just in love,
Which explains why at midnight, only around you does it seem like the
    sun's come up,
Since that night I've been thinking if in terms of love there's ever such
    thing as too much,
Like I imagined being pummeled by millions of your kisses, unable to
    decide when enough was enough,
And as crazy as I may be for saying this, I feel no shame,
I would follow you to the end of the world,
Even if you decided to jump off,
I would jump in front of a firing squad for a head start on protecting you
    from above,
And I would do all these irrational things in the name of love unable to
    see error,
Because I want you to stay by my side forever,
It's a cold December, so I was wondering if you could let me hold you tight,
Hopefully, you'll hear this message blowing through the wind during the
    sunrise

When I hear the word fairytale I think of words like happily ever after,
I remember things like Santa Claus and the Easter Bunny aren't real,
    which would mean happiness never does come after,
And then I met you,
I look into your eyes and see a world I never knew,
It made me realize I've been looking down for so long that I forgot the
    sky was blue,
I remembered that I was supposed to wake up and smell the roses,
I forgot about troubles in my past life and finally remembered what home is,
Let's be honest and ask ourselves who would've thought I'd get a girl
    like you,
A nerdy guy with decent looks being around a girl as magnificent as you,
    it's almost disgraceful,
I'm going to jump back a few lines to tell you how I found out what home is,
Home is where the heart is, so for a body builder, home would be a place
    of fitness,
But after being out of the house for about twenty minutes I realized my
    heart was with you,
We don't see the same thing, because I think I'm fat, and with that being
    said, your presence is the best food,
I'm starting to run out of ideas and the only thought I'm having is of you,
I know you're tired of going through the same old thing, but I'm not here
    to make you feel seduced,
I'm here because I couldn't go to college to pursue my career of getting
    married to you,
And I almost forgot what love was until butterflies flew around my stom-
    ach when you entered my view,
All I ask for is the chance to make everything right,
I want our love to represent love and not about who can fight,
I want to travel the world with you since I seem to fall for you endlessly,

I never would've guessed that I would've gotten goose bumps or felt my
   whole body tingling,
It was like a magnetic attraction created by Mother Nature, brought you
   to me,
What I'm trying to say is I like the way you look, and the way you make
   me feel,
I like the way you talk, so allow me to walk you down this aisle so you
   can know it's real,
I hope my words impressed you enough because with you I hope for time-
   less memories,
You are the best decision I've made in life, and I never would've guessed
   I'd ask this, but will you marry me?

If you really love me, can you say it now,
I feel like you do but I'm terrible at figuring these things out,
I want to hear you say it,
But only if it's the truth,
Because I'm trying to be patient, but I can't pretend I don't want you,
I remember the first time I felt your touch because it was the only night
 I slept through,
When I was in your arms, I felt something I believed to be impossible,
So, when I tell you I need you every second of the day, believe me when
 I say it,
The thought of being with you is the most precious thing ever and I'd
 never replace it,
Because when I was inside your arms, I felt love,
But this one had various kinds of capabilities,
It almost felt as if it was created to be the perfect fit for me,
And when I tell you it was the most amazing feeling,
I mean I could've stayed there forever,
It's the best feeling in the world when we come together,
Personally, I think you're something special, and even though right now
 may not be the right time,
Seeing you is the only reason I believe in love at first sight,
Because when I saw you, I was lifted by these butterflies,
I convinced myself I had a staring problem because you were the only
 thing my eyes could find,
Truth is, I was wondering if you wanted to run and be together for the
 rest of our lives

I'm not sure what it is that you did to me,
But there's something about the love you give that makes me weak,
And if this world were mine, you could have anything,
I would make sure the most beautiful flowers it has to offer would rest at
    your feet,
And you would rest your head on the finest of all bed sheets,
I would hold on to you ever so tight, because if this world were mine,
    you could take it from me,
Being loved by you puts the world in a whole different light,
And as unbelievable as it may sound, I fall in love every time you look
    into my eyes,
Because even single moment with you gives me the best sensation,
It makes writing about love so effortless by removing all expectations,
When I feel at my lowest, I write about you because you are my inspiration,
Just the thought of you clears my mind and removes hesitation,
I just love you so much I couldn't say it with a boring message,
So, I'm here writing if this world were mine that way you can know
    where my head is,
And if this world were mine, you would have more than just the birds
    and the bees,
This world is mine and I want it to be yours, which is why I'm down on
    one knee,
So, since the world is mine, I'm going to get rid of the clouds so the sky
    can forever be blue,
I plan to add an eighth wonder that's more beautiful than the other seven,
And even if nobody else could believe something ever that is ever so true,
The eighth wonder is the center of my world,
And I guess I could take these hints away to finally say this eighth wonder
    would be you

It was just a kiss that we shared, or maybe that's just how it seemed,
Not to me,
Only to the people around us because to me it meant everything,
And it wasn't just the first one it was all the kisses that came with it,
Our lips touched, and the soul transfer began,
I felt myself enter your body with a pleasure that was better than anything
    I felt sexually,
Plus, I remember the time you looked me in the eyes and said it was the
    little things,
The first kiss was the perfect out-of-body experience,
Whenever our lips separated, space became something I could see,
Because you elevated me beyond the heavens,
And I wonder if you feel it too, because zero gravity feels amazing,
The trees turned greener than they've ever been and everything else came
    to life,
But it was just a kiss,
Not the first one, but every one that came after,
Every time my world was shared, and our souls were hugging in the sky,
So, it wasn't just a kiss to me,
And the butterflies in my stomach weren't just butterflies,
They were the signs that I found my wife,
The woman He put on the earth for me

Late at night,
Whenever I find myself thinking about you the most it's late at night,
I mean like it's far beyond the p.m. hours, it's like, *why you up so late,*
But it's the most peaceful time because when I look out the window I can
    see your face,
I mean, sure, it's three o'clock in the morning,
But something about seeing you then feels so right,
It's almost like an open the window to figure out if I can fly,
Late at night,
I was lying in bed worrying if the bed you're sleeping on is just as
    comfortable,
Honestly, I'm worrying if your headspace is good because I want to
    comfort you,
We should consider this time early morning, but I'm waiting for your kiss
    goodnight,
I'm starting to learn that I can't sleep the same when you aren't by my side,
I wanted to let you know I'm saving up money so we can get a big book
    for our photo collection,
But I want to fill it with mostly pictures of you and our kids whenever
    we get them,
Late at night,
Unfortunately, I woke up to realize that you were never actually here,
It was the best dream I ever had,
And now I've opened my eyes to a nightmare,
It's okay I left my heart back in that dream with you,
Because they always told me if you can think of something, somebody
    else has too,
So now I'm hoping you are a real person, and you feel the same way I do,
That way my dreams can stop being lucid and they can just be true
Late at night I realized my heart will forever belong to one person,
Tonight, I found out that person was you

I want you to love me naked,
The last person I gave my heart to turned out to be a demon,
So, the moment I turned my back they went to trade it,
I searched for love in characteristics that come from a mother figure,
Because if love were an anchor attached to my ankle, she'd still say I'm
 the strongest swimmer,
And I wonder why she did it,
I mean I wonder why she had to lie to me,
I accepted her for whatever she came with,
But didn't know she lacked honesty,
I want you to love me naked,
And I'm hoping it stays the same even when the burns heal,
As a child I had enemies in CPS because we were in the same room when
 they went to kill,
And I figured I should let you know my heart is broke,
Because nobody else spared time to show change,
And I feel like I had to let you know because I've been let down by the
 ones I needed most,
I want you to love me naked,
I want you to come around, learn who I am, and take care of my broken
 piece, not replace it

They told me love is one of the strongest drugs, warning me not to take too much,
I'm not going to lie here admitting I got a taste without knowing if there was enough,
So later I'll be going back to be with her because I can't wait to feel her touch,
It was that split second when my smile meant something that I knew there was no chance of growing up,
Because I start acting like a child the moment, I truly feel like I'm in love,
I'll get on your nerves more than anything, but I'll be here whenever times get rough,
I'm the type to hear you want something and get it for you while finding out how to make ends meet,
I don't talk much, but if you ask the people around me, I'm kind of funny,
And since we are standing here, I figured I'd let you know we are past the petty arguments,
I fully stand behind communication even though our emotions will get sparked a little bit,
The kind of man I am will allow me to love you however you need as long as you tell me how,
You'll never be able to do wrong in my eyes because with my love there's always a way around,
I'm proud to show you off, and I'm more than willing to shout your name in the valley,
And I would love if you showed the world how much you love me,
My love language is touch, and I don't believe there's such thing as being too close,
If you ever said that home is where the heart is, then there's no other place for us to go,
At night I don't sleep because I spend that time wondering if I ever cross your mind,
When we meet, I hope you feel the same way because I'm ready for the best times of my life

I'm not particularly good at this love poem thing,
But I thought about you, so I figured I'd draft a poem that meant something,
The kind that you don't have to think about,
But it just makes your ears ring,
And if I were going to write a love poem, it would go like this,
Love has a sound,
It sounds exactly like your snore,
I mean I heard it in my ear the other night,
Actually, it might sound more like your laugh,
I really can't tell I just know that you never leave my mind,
In fact, I was supposed to give you a ticket because there was a stop sign,
But love has a sound and it's quite romantic,
Love is a drug, and you can't overdose if you don't panic,
And you make me think about the things I say because they must be perfect,
Like you're worth more than just a bouquet of roses,
Because I can think of more than twelve reasons why you make me nervous,
But love has a sound,
It's faint, and I think I can only hear it when you're around

25

And I'm talking like the light never shined,
Or if this camera can't hold anymore footage,
I figured before you walk away, I can give one more demonstration,
To speak the final words about myself I always thought I couldn't,
And to be honest with you, opening up makes me nervous,
But because I'm scared of love, I tend to ruin relations,
The way my mind looks at love is the same as how the world will look
    down upon racists,
And Mom, these are the times I realize how much I need you,
Not just to show me how tough love is but how you satisfy a sweet tooth,
What you're not understanding is the last person lied to me after I gave
    them everything,
And will come back around once I feel like there's a better me,
So, when I say I need you around I mean that I hope you never decide to
    leave,
Her and I went from talking about future plans to wondering if today's
    the day we decide to speak,
I want you to love me naked,
Because my words will say *go away* while my heart screams *I hope we*
    make it

I want you to love me naked,
And when I say that I'm talking beyond what you see,
Not just the guy with decent looks and make-shift waves in his head,
Or as the semi-buff guy who has a few tattoos,
I want you to love me naked,
I'm talking no clothes on with the lights turned off,
And beyond the words in this poem,
For me it's deeper than every scar you see,
To love me correctly you must look at the dust inside of the bones that
    lie underneath,
My heartbeat sounds like a baby's cry, whether or not you believe it,
The only person who wakes up is me as the parent, so I don't sleep, for
    good reasons,
But I want you to love me naked,
Whether it's on the front page of a magazine,
Or a crooked smile without the desire for braces,
The truth is, I want you to love me for me,
This is the inside of my love life, so please pay attention to my story

The feeling inside my heart has only been felt by those who rest above,

Here I want to introduce you to myself along with this feeling that's beyond love,

I'm not much of a love poet, but hopefully these words grasp your soul in a million hugs,

Because if love is truly the strongest one ever, I might have found the deadliest drug,

I believe love is something known to the world specifically to recreate what we consider to be a comfort zone,

And you'll never know how good it feels till the man becomes the child while the woman remains the mother,

Otherwise known as what it looks like when they're comfortable,

Hello, my name is Byron,

Feel free to kick your shoes off and take this heart of mine as a reminder that you're no longer alone,

I'm not sure if you'll remember me, although the thought of you will have me taking the long way home,

The second we leave there's a ninety percent chance I'll go out of my way just to see where you go,

I'm not going to follow you home or anything,

This is how my mind creates a memory while my heart is hoping there will be another time we're able to get this close,

I'm not much of a love poet, nor am I a magician, but I'll find a way to get rid of your past memories,

Allowing me to show you that love isn't what you had I'll make it look differently

*Okay, I don't like the way you walk, you talk funny, your teeth have a lot
of plaque buildup, and I think you're ugly,*
Sorry for the sudden outburst, but I figured since they filled your past,
    I'd tell any lie I could before I show you the real me,
They're all just corny insults, like how your makeup color doesn't match
    or how sometimes your breath smells so good I don't think you brush
    your teeth,
Wait, that one didn't make any sense, but what I'm saying is it's hard to
    make up flaws for a person who doesn't have any,
If your hair didn't smell like the ocean breeze, I'd assume the products
    you used were Garnier Fructis,
I'm not any good with hair products, so I guess you can imagine taking
    a dot of anything and applying it to this hair you can barely see,
But if your smile didn't make a hotel pillow look like it came from Wal-
    mart, I would think you use Sensodyne

You know,

The other day I decided to make a stalker-like move and search the inter-
net to find a picture of you so I can do this project about my dreams,

I know I could've gone to Instagram and found a picture, but I know the
best things in life never come easy,

So, the other night I thought I'm overqualified to be your boyfriend and
I've got a list of three reasons in case you were wondering,

One, the terms were to stay solid during tough times and love you un-
conditionally,

I've been doing that for months now, so, with no title, I've covered the
most important thing,

Two, I heard your ex got around, so now your biggest fear is loyalty,

I refuse to turn my back on you, so the foundation of my loyalty is con-
crete,

Three, when I thought about introducing you as my girl, my heart ran a
marathon before coming back to me,

Four, giving you attention and showing you my love is something I could
do day in and day out every week,

Five, I should say five reasons because now I'm thinking and reasons are
coming faster than masked men after a robbery,

Maybe I'm overqualified to be your man, but I love making people smile,
and after seeing yours I want to pursue a career in comedy,

The first time you said hi to me my cheeks turned as red as a peach and
the overproduction of saliva made it hard to speak,

I may be overqualified to be your man, but that doesn't mean you aren't
the person I want here with me

You're beautiful, magnificent, fluorescent, astonishing, and the most important of all you're what the world means to me,
Your smile reminds me of every sunrise scene embracing love in the most romantic movies,
I was asked to describe you in four words, so I chose to use "the world to me,"
And even during the times where the sun doesn't shine you help me to see,
Mistakes in the past have changed us both for the better, but I think it's time I use you to occupy the hole in my heart where loved used to be,
I never wrote a good love poem before, but I imagine that my love poem would sound like your heartbeat,
I imagine it would make the ironically compared thumping that doesn't force kids to run down the street,
And that's because when I think of love, I picture things like love and basketball, where the support of somebody's passion took them to the moon,
I picture the impossibly perfect painting of how beautiful the sunset looks when you sit on the beach in the late afternoon,
When I think of a love poem, I think it's supposed to contain how strongly you feel about somebody,
But I don't think the world's strongest man could lift this pen,
Because the strength it requires to live this pen is like Thor's hammer,
Only the purest heart could raise it in the end,

That didn't illustrate what it's supposed to mean, but to summarize, having you by my side is a dream,
But this isn't the one I want to wake out of because I'd rather live in the middle of the ocean than watch you leave

Roses are red,
Violets are blue,
I believe in romance,
And it all started with you,
Because it wasn't until the thought of you that I saw the sun and the moon,
It was dawn and it taught me two different souls could calmly occupy the
    same room,
Not in compliance,
It was like they mended together forming something ever so beautiful,
And in this I started believing that we could do it too,
From my looks and the way my character is you probably think I'm too
    silly to know anything about love,
What I can tell you is I'm great at writing my emotions out, yet my love
    language is touch,
From the moment I looked into your eyes I fell deep in this place where
    the sky was red; it was so beautiful, I hope you can come,
We can escape this cold reality, and if we stay on schedule, we can still
    catch the sun,
You are the most beautiful person my eyes have ever seen and there's not
    a picture or video that can change the words that I've said,
I've fallen deep in love with you and now it's gotten to the point where
    my heart has taken over my head,
The other night my heart told me that we can still be lovers and friends,
Because now when I think of romance, I picture sunsets and picnics,
I think of deep conversations with you and ten thousand kisses,
It's way more exciting than butterflies because I'm turning into a reindeer
    on Christmas,
I'm at your every demand because my goal is to grant all your wishes,
It was you who elevated my mind beyond paradise, and I still don't know
    what this is,
Like who even roller blades anymore or wants to drive around to some
    R&B,

I want to travel the world because the girl of my dreams is right there
    with me,
I got a whole bunch of dress clothes in my closet with some fresh flowers
    waiting for a night out with you,
Because I was built for this life consisting of showing what love really is
    to you,
I want to ask that you let me in your heart, but don't you dare forget me,
I'm still holding these flowers, and I'm hoping you grab them soon be-
    cause my palms getting itchy

Faceless Love

Your eyes say things I never hear from you,
The crazy part is they say exactly how I feel and I'm wondering if it's true,
I guess what I'm trying to say is,
I love you,
I've felt this for a long time, but I could never find the courage to tell you,
But it played out like a movie even though I was shy,
In my head I looked at you, fell in love, and you chose me over every
    other guy,
It was like the stars aligned and I was given a second chance at love,
Instantly, I knew I would ride for you even after the wheels fell off,
I would follow you deep into the ocean or to the skies above,
You are the best creation that was ever made by God,
And I feel crazy for asking this,
But can I come home for just one night,
Because they always said home is where the heart is and mine is at your side,
I just want one night to place you in my arms and hold you super tight,
And there's no such thing as darkness now that you're around,
So would you mind being the lady in my life,
I just know that if you let me in your heart, you'll forget what it's like to
    be cold,
Your beauty is ageless, and I don't think you'll even have a wrinkle in
    your skin when your ninety years old,
Because this love we share is amazing and it could keep us young forever,
I saw it all in a dream once, and all it took was this one night for us to be
    together,
Unbelievably, this is love at first sight,
So now you can only imagine how I feel after learning you were more
    than just a face,
I dreamt a wild dream once before, and somehow in the end we shared a
    last name

I need you every day,
And I hope you believe the words I have to say,
Because I whispered your name into the wind,
I'm not sure what I was hoping to accomplish, although it felt like I was
    speaking you into existence,
I used to question it before, but I knew the moment I felt your touch,
It was no longer a goodbye hug,
It was the night I fell in love,
It was the sparkle in your eyes that caressed my soul for the first time
    since I was young,
And suddenly I was lost in a movie called *Love Jones*, remembering love,
I remembered the nights falling asleep to the sound of your voice before
    the scene changed,
I fell in love with the way you smiled when I asked for an even exchange,
Because it was the first time somebody was willing to give you their heart
    and soul,
So, tonight, if I can get a hold of your soul, I promise to never let it go,
It wasn't until you walked away that being alone felt so lonely,
I tossed and turned all night because the possibility of not seeing you
    makes it hard to sleep,
And whenever I try to think of a life without us, I must get my inhaler
    just so I can breathe,
What I think you should know is that I've never been good when it comes
    to compliments,
But one thing I can say with all the belief in my heart is that you are a
    godsend,
The other night you had left, and right after the door closed, the room had
    no oxygen,
It's your smile that has me writing crazy things with such confidence,
And it's your love that makes me feel whole in a way nobody else ever did

I met you when the world was looking dark,
You were this walking light that told me it was too soon to give up,
All you did was smile, and I felt like I was enough,
I remember standing there, waiting for the day they finally set me free,
I've been waiting for decades to see the day I'm free of all these past
    tragedies,
I'm not sure if you remember, but I first saw you on the other side of the
    room,
I knew I loved you at that moment and I wanted to let it be known,
But reality hit me before I could open my mouth because it was too soon,
When I looked into your eyes was the first time I ever felt at home,
And one day I'll be your knight in shining armor; I saw it written in stone,
So, one day I'm hoping I can know everything about you that way I can
    attach my soul,
Because love at first sight with a soul tie, aw man you best believe I won't
    let go,
It's been a few nights since I've slept,
But honestly, I was wondering if you were thinking the same thing,
If you, are I'm still waiting for you to text me,
What I meant to say was there's no question whether I'm in love with you,
I feel like I fall in love with you every day and it hits me like a typhoon,
And I'm learning how to fly again so I need an angel like you to teach
    me how to use my wings,
Forever hasn't been forever in a long time so let me introduce you to an
    eternity

I know Tinkerbell isn't real, but she taught me to always keep belief,
So, I believe one day you'll see how much more I care about you than
    anybody else you know because I know what it means,
I know the truth hurts, but if you were to say no right now, I would try
    again next week,
I know what it means to say you love somebody and mean every syllable
    of the phrase, because to gain your love, I would let my heart bleed,
I don't think Romeo and Juliet were meant to be, but I've seen a lot of
    toxic things,
But if being in love is like drinking poison, then I'll consume however
    much I please,
I'm asking if you'll take my hand because even though life isn't a musi-
    cal, I want you to save that last dance for me,
Yes, that was a reference to a 2001 movie,
And I'm terrible at keeping my own balance, though I promise I can
    sweep you off your feet,
They should call me Meg in *Hercules*, the Disney cartoon, because I
    won't say I'm in love until you say it to me,
Or because I died inside of a tomb like King Tut, but you held so much
    love for me that our children's children will have me as a memory,
Now I never wrote a love poem, but I imagine it would sound like love's
    fun to do,
I think my love poem would sound like that time late at night when our
    sleepy voices spill the words *I love you,*

Basically my love poem sounds like this,

Roses are red and violets are blue,

The thought of you never leaves my head,

So, I wanted to take this time to ask if you'll make my dream come true

My heart beating out of my chest,
My hands and feet covered with sweat,
And the discomfort of carpet rubbing against my leg,
To think this was the recipe for hope that you say yes,
I guess I never really got the opportunity to tell you how I really feel,
So I'll take my heart and squeeze it into this envelope for you to reveal,
The truth is that I will sound crazy if I really explain what it came to be,
When I first saw you, it became the first out-of-body experience for me,
Like I was awake at nighttime, somehow still seeing you in my dreams,
But I guess that's normal, because you see a rainbow when it rains,
It's just that split moment when you finally feel like everything will be okay,
So now when I look into your eyes, my heart finds peace without pain,
Separation was to cause us the most of problems although the love shall
     not change,
And it kills me that you wonder why I stare for so long when I see your face,
You are the one my heart cried for, and there is no debate,
Showing me what love really feels like now we're engaged,
You may not completely understand but life hit me hard,
And for years I thought of myself as some kind of mistake,
Then I met you,
And every time I hear your voice, I forget that pain has a name,
Whenever I get bored, I look at picture of you, hoping that you're forever
     kept safe,
I don't think you understand what it's like having your soul leave your body,
I'm hoping these words blow up on your mind because you're the special
     somebody,
Being with you I feel so high in the clouds that there's no GPS that could
     find me,
This is only the beginning of what I have to say because you'll never
     quite know what you did to me,
Seeing you in front of me feels like an epiphany,
The out-of-body experience are the words I use to describe how I'm feeling

I fell in love with the sight of you,

I began to indulge in your love to find out you were more than just a beautiful face,

You were someone I could love until our skin turned wrinkly and our hair gray,

And if I remember one thing at all,

It's how hard I would dream of something like this as a kid,

The moment somebody acknowledged me for who I am and accepted it,

And I always told myself that if I were ever to fall in love it would be just like this,

I said if I ever fell in love my confession would sound like the most beautiful sunrises,

It would be as secure as the white house and full of happiness,

We have the best times together because we're not only lovers we're also best friends,

And for the longest time I didn't know what she looked like, but I knew she was true,

When I reminisce about these dreams now the woman who's there looks just like you,

And I believe in the impossible,

But I don't think I'd mistake the most beautiful woman I've ever seen,

I'd never forget seeing every wonder in the world inside of a human being,

I remember the feeling and how my heart skipped six beats,

It jumped up, down, then to the right four times before opening,

In case you don't remember, that's the combination you set on it when you locked it away,

Knowing my love was meant strictly for you as it grows more every day,

I just wanted to let you know I love you in the cleverest way I could find,

Tonight, if there's one thing I know for sure it's that I want you to be the lady of my life

I wrote this at a stoplight,
And to no avail, I did this thinking about you,
I looked in the sky and your smile had replaced the moon,
The music in the car had a lot more rhythm leaving behind the blues,
And in these two minutes I wondered if you know anything regarding the
    way God and I talk about you,
After the light turns green, I concluded that there's no way you even had
    a clue,
Because my heart tells me that if there was the slightest chance that you
    knew,
You would feel exactly how I do,
Because I felt love for the first time when I lied next to you,
I remember because on that night the stars were shining awfully bright,
I couldn't look in the sky for too long without it hurting, which caused
    me to get lost in your eyes,
And the second I caught a glimpse of your soul my mind told me to swal-
    low my pride,
So now I'm here waiting for a green light on the intersection of sunset
    and paradise,
Thinking of a million diverse ways to ask you to never swallow the
    thought of walking away,
I'm not sure what you did to me, but now I don't think I'll ever be too
    proud to beg,
The best way to explain it to you is that for me to breathe properly, it re-
    quires you to stay,
It was the sound of your voice that made me feel like a bag of sand re-
    placed my legs,

To me you're not just another person, you truly are something special,
When I was a kid, I always told myself that if I ever found a love like
    this I would never let go,
I love everything about you, especially how perfectly your smile sits on
    your face,
You are the most beautiful wonder in the world that time could never steal
    away,
Well, the police officers have pulled up beside me, so I guess I should
    tuck my phone away,
I wrote this at a stoplight thinking of the time we spent yesterday

So, she asked me to open up,
I figured I should, so I told her let's go for a ride,
We may not be in the same state, but I need you to see these city lights,
Because what they do for this city, you do for my entire life,
When you're around everything becomes beautiful, although there's
    never enough time,
Time for me to absorb your essence, because the moment you leave, I
    may not feel all right,
In this calligram you may not physically see the picture when the words
    spiral around my mind,
My first question to you is *do you love me,*
Not the obvious yes or no, just what you're feeling spiritually,
This feeling is more than just love because it has my mind running around
    the ceiling,
And this heartbeat in my chest feels like somewhere inside there's a
    trampoline,
Because I am a man with a lot to learn; I just want to make sure you hear me,
I want to make sure you hear me clearly when I say I love you dearly,
The second question I wonder is if you realized I love the way you look
    in my eyes,
Not just before the kiss but more like every time our time together creates
    this vibe,
Because for me it came like a wave,
And I'm a California baby so I hopped on my surfboard as I was raised
    to the sky,
Shortly after realizing that it was the moment you said hi that created this
    high,

I can't paint this whole picture in one poem, so maybe I'll make another
     to keep it complete,
Because you are me, and I am you, so together We Are Peace
I don't necessarily think there's a statement that involves the things I have
to say,
I want to say, what's a day without the sun, but I don't think that'll come
     off the right way,
But what if I were to tell you, you mean more to me than you know,
Or if I said that you make me feel like a million different things, although
     I thought it was impossible,
I…feel like I can't really put the words to really fit what you mean to me,
I want to say that your value to me is the same as the suns to the trees,
Or to make a cliché phrase like something about honey to bees,
Just being in your presence makes me feel like a prisoner who just got
     set free,
With you I finally feel like I have the chance to wake up and just breathe,
But somehow after saying all of that I still feel like my message is in-
     complete,
There's just so much I must tell you and I can't wait until the sun goes down,
I don't see the point in acting like children who still must sneak out of
     the house,
There's just…. There's a piece of me that just always wants you around,
What you mean to me is equal to how much music needs sound,
Before I see the moon, I must make sure the sun shines until you see what
     I mean,
Money makes the world go round and I feel like you're both money and
     the whole world to me,
You're meaning to me is like crime and the police,
Because even if I say I don't want you around, I'm glad you always keep
     me busy,

Would it come off better if I were to ask what a wedding would be without
	a ring,
Or how great of a kingdom a king would run without having a queen,
Is the best way to put it to say that I need you the way a relationship needs
	loyalty?
Is it wrong to say that love is war so we should act like we hate each other,
	and both be casualties?
Look…. What I'm trying to tell you is that to me you mean more than
	the world I live on, the water I drink, and the food I need to eat,
To me you mean love, happiness, sadness, and anger, which would be
	about everything,
To me you mean a breath of fresh air, a drink of icy water, and about any
	idea in between,
To me you represent my heart, my brain, my life, and my death, so take
	the most important thing to you, multiply it by a billion, and that's
	what you mean to me

Hello, can you help me, I'm falling in love for the first time,
I've been arguing with myself for weeks and I need you to catch me be-
    cause when I read about love, all I see is blurred lines,
And I like your smile a lot, in case I failed to mention that, I've been lost
    in it for weeks,
I have bad knees so I put a couple braces on and, the same way you use
    them to straighten out teeth, I think you could straighten out me,
It's too early to say it but I want you to know who I am and how I became
    this way over the years,
I want to put my life story in your hands and express myself to the fullest
    while holding back the tears,
And I'm falling but I couldn't tell you how far,
I'm falling into this hole called love because I asked God where my heart
    was and he told me I'll find it wherever you are,
I've been drafting my story for so long but I'm missing the pages that in-
    volve my encounter with you and how it changed my life,
Being with you, I learned that love is more than just a title, so allow me
    to give you my heart because I just want to be right by your side,
So, I look in your eyes and I tell you that I'd do the same for you, because
    love doesn't come with a mystery, we'll leave that for Scooby Doo,
I understand that your last may have done you wrong, but if you read this
    closely, you'll see that I'm all about you,
I want to be the one you come home to, just so I could show you that the
    world I'll create for you is bigger than Neptune,
And even though your ring won't match Saturn's, I want you to recognize
    the pattern of how I stop your heart from turning blue,
As terrible as it sounds, I want to share my demons so they can help me
    explain the reasons why at times I can be obsessed with myself,

I tried telling you a few things before I learned that all I must do is talk,
    because you know me better than I know myself,
I want to sit next to you as we both learn what being in love really means,
Can you catch me because between you and I, I put my last dollar as a
    down payment on our dreams,
As weird as it may sound, when you're asleep I hear the angels singing
    extremely loud,
Because you bring me into heaven with you when you return home, and
    every time I hear you snore, it makes my soul smile,
At the beginning I asked you to catch me, but I didn't mean it because
    I'm falling in love, I needed an excuse to be in your arms,
Because at that moment, and that moment only, I finally felt like I wasn't
    going to fall apart

It's been a while since you felt special, hasn't it,
The last thing you had couldn't compare to this,
Only my words will let you know exactly what you are,
The actions come later, they stay nowhere, far,
To me there's a different meaning of special,
I'd say it's something that has a meaning depending on your view,
The most important thing to me as of recently became you,
The things you do always come with a different feeling,
Simple things like buying food come with a whole different meaning,
If it has your name attached to it, the value changes,
I learned after a while those good things do come with patience,
Allow me to explain to you exactly what I'm attempting to prove,
My head spends a lot of time in dark places, but you're a good muse,
Your smile makes my heart drop, and the world doesn't move,
I get lost in something so beautiful I forget what I was trying to do,
And to simply describe the feeling I get looking into your eyes,
Half of the time you don't remember when you're hypnotized,
Yet when I'm looking, I know exactly where to go,
I barely got a taste, but I fell in love with your soul,
Notice how every time I look past your looks,
Somebody wanting to take care of you emotionally has you shook,
I want to support you not only physically but mentally too,
A three-letter word that means everything to me is you

A faceless love,
I remember the first time we met,
You were merely a shadow then,
I was a young teen with a dream of love far beyond establishment,
It was dark when I met you,
But it was the way you felt that I will never forget,
Because i fell subject to a dance and the floor felt like rose petals,
It was much more than a soul tie and this time I won't let go,
I remember how you held me,
It was the same way my mom held us after we got cold playing in the
    snow,
I would hold your hand if mine didn't begin to sweat every time I got
    nervous,
Only when I'm around you does my body feel like some kind of furnace,
I remember when I tried to kiss you and realized this whole time you did-
    n't have a face,
You were still yet to be a person and the red dress was something I started
    to hallucinate,
But I remember how the moon shined behind us the moment we began
    to dance,
A faceless love represents someone I have yet to find,
While still drowning in thoughts of romance